Patrick Mahomes

I0878798

Patrick Mahomes

MVP QUARTERBACK WHO GIVES BACK

J. G. Minyard

LERNER PUBLICATIONS ◆ MINNEAPOLIS

Lerner Publications Company
An imprint of Lerner Publishing Group, Inc.
241 First Avenue North
Minneapolis, MN 55401 USA

For reading levels and more information, look up this title at www.lernerbooks.com.

Main body text set in Rotis Serif Std 55 Regular. Typeface provided by Adobe Systems.

Editor: Ashley Kuehl

Library of Congress Cataloging-in-Publication Data

Names: Minyard, J. G., author.
Title: Patrick Mahomes : MVP quarterback who gives back / J. G. Minyard.
Description: Minneapolis, MN : Lerner Publications, [2026] | Series: Gateway biographies | Includes bibliographical references and index. | Audience: Ages 9–14 | Audience: Grades 4–6 | Summary: "Readers explore the life of Patrick Mahomes II, quarterback for the Kansas City Chiefs. Discover his fascinating journey from humble beginnings in Texas all the way to leading his team to back-to-back Super Bowl victories"– Provided by publisher.
Identifiers: LCCN 2025001496 (print) | LCCN 2025001497 (ebook) | ISBN 9798765669372 (library binding) | ISBN 9798765684122 (paperback) | ISBN 9798765677537 (epub)
Subjects: LCSH: Mahomes, Patrick, 1995–-Juvenile literature. | Kansas City Chiefs (Football team)–Juvenile literature. | Quarterbacks (Football)–United States–Biography–Juvenile literature. | Football players–United States–Biography–Juvenile literature.
Classification: LCC GV939.M284 M56 2025 (print) | LCC GV939.M284 (ebook) | DDC 796.332092 [B]–dc23/eng/20250127

LC record available at https://lccn.loc.gov/2025001496
LC ebook record available at https://lccn.loc.gov/2025001497

Manufactured in the United States of America
1-1012013-53908-3/24/2025

TABLE OF CONTENTS

The Kansas City Chiefs face off against the San Francisco 49ers at the start of Super Bowl LIV on February 2, 2020.

On February 2, 2020, Patrick Mahomes and the Kansas City Chiefs were trying to win their first Super Bowl in 50 years. Fans poured into Hard Rock Stadium in Miami Gardens, Florida, to watch Kansas City face off against the San Francisco 49ers. As the game entered the fourth quarter, the 49ers had a strong lead. The score was 20–10, and Kansas City quarterback Patrick Mahomes had thrown two passes that were intercepted by the defense.

National Football League (NFL) fans around the world were beginning to think the 49ers might win. But Mahomes thought differently. "We never lost faith," Mahomes later said. "That's the biggest thing. Everybody on this team, no one had their head down. We believed in each other. That's what we preached all year long."

Knowing Kansas City's season was on the line, Mahomes threw long passes with incredible accuracy,

Mahomes throws a pass during the 2020 Super Bowl game against the San Francisco 49ers.

including a 44-yard pass to teammate Tyreek Hill. In moments where he couldn't find an open teammate, Mahomes even rushed the defense himself, sprinting between defenders to get closer to the end zone. When Mahomes finally zipped a pass to Travis Kelce for the touchdown, the score was 20–16, and Kansas City was back in the game.

Through clever passes and quick rushes, Kansas City made their way to the end zone again, where a quick pass from Mahomes to Damien Williams resulted in another touchdown. The score was 23–20, and Kansas City had finally taken the lead.

While San Francisco tried their hardest to retake

the lead, Kansas City managed to score yet another touchdown in the final seconds of the game. The final score was 31–20, and Kansas City had won their first Super Bowl game in 50 years.

As confetti rained down across the football field, Mahomes was awarded the Super Bowl Most Valuable Player (MVP) award for leading the team with his clever passes and clutch decision-making. When he was interviewed after the game, Mahomes said he planned to celebrate by fulfilling his lifelong dream of going to Disney World. At twenty-four years old, he was the youngest quarterback and the second Black quarterback

Mahomes cheers after the Chiefs score a touchdown in the 2020 Super Bowl game against the 49ers.

to receive the MVP award in NFL history. At the end of the interview, Mahomes thanked the interviewer before grabbing the mic to shout, “Kansas City, we did it, baby!” Nobody knew it yet, but this historic Super Bowl win would be one of many for Patrick Mahomes and the Kansas City Chiefs.

THE PATH TO GREATNESS

Patrick Lavon Mahomes II was born on September 17, 1995, in Tyler, Texas. He was mostly raised by his mother, Randi Martin Mahomes. Patrick’s father, Pat Mahomes, was a professional baseball pitcher who played 11 seasons with Major League Baseball (MLB) teams. Patrick grew up living with one brother. He also has a half brother and two half sisters.

Though Patrick’s parents divorced when he was young, both parents remained in his life. Like Patrick, all his siblings play sports. His younger sisters, Mia Randall and Zoe Mahomes, both play multiple sports including basketball and soccer. His younger brother Graham Walker played football for Brown University and Rice University. No matter the sport, the Mahomes family loves an athletic competition.

As a young boy, Patrick sometimes went to work with his father, where MLB greats such as Alex Rodriguez and Derek Jeter gave him tips on how to be a better baseball player. From a young age, Patrick was set up for success.

PATRICK MAHOMES I

Patrick (Pat) Mahomes I, father of famous quarterback Patrick Mahomes II, was born in Bryan, Texas, in 1970. Long before his quarterback son was born, Pat was a professional baseball pitcher. He played for the Pittsburgh Pirates, New York Mets, Chicago Cubs, Minnesota Twins, Texas Rangers, and Boston Red Sox.

Like his son, Pat enjoyed playing basketball, baseball, and football. He was so good at the sports he played, he received college scholarships for each one! He rejected his scholarships when the Minnesota Twins drafted him to play baseball professionally. The elder Mahomes retired from professional sports in 2009. These days, he's often seen attending his son's football games.

Pat Mahomes pitches for the Minnesota Twins in 1994.

Mahomes threw all his energy into honing his skills as a quarterback at Texas Tech.

But even as he wowed people with his impressive throwing arm and baseball skills, young Patrick already had his eyes on football. His favorite team growing up was the Dallas Cowboys, and he was a big fan of Dallas quarterback Tony Romo. When he was young, Patrick had many talents. He was so gifted athletically that his father nicknamed him Showtime.

Patrick attended Whitehouse High School in Whitehouse, Texas, where he was not only an impressive football player but also an excellent basketball and baseball player. It was at Whitehouse High School that he met Brittany Matthews, whom he would later marry. In high school, Patrick was a terrific baseball pitcher. He even threw an impressive 16-strikeout no-hitter in his senior year of high school.

He was so good at his other sports, his father encouraged him to quit football altogether! His father later told newspapers, "I just thought we were wasting time when he could have been working on the sports he would go to college for, baseball and basketball. Plus, I didn't want him to get hurt."

Patrick didn't take that piece of advice, and he continued playing football. Using the skills he'd gained from basketball and baseball, the young athlete had a terrific high school football career, throwing for 4,619 yards, throwing 50 touchdown passes, and rushing for almost 1,200 yards. When it came to sports, Patrick was great at everything he tried. In fact, he was so good, it became a problem.

A DIFFICULT CHOICE

After Mahomes graduated from high school in 2014, he was faced with a difficult choice. That year, when the athlete was 19 years old, the Detroit Tigers drafted him to play baseball professionally. If he chose to skip college, he could have been a professional baseball player right after high school! But Mahomes loved playing football. He decided to commit to playing at Texas Tech University while he got his degree.

At first, Mahomes played both baseball and football for Texas Tech. But eventually he decided to quit baseball and focused on becoming the best quarterback he could be.

Despite his terrific high school success, Mahomes

Mahomes played for Texas Tech from 2014 through 2016.

didn't get much playing time at the beginning. But a big chance came during his freshman year. Future professional quarterback Davis Webb was the team's usual starter. But after Webb suffered an injury that left him on crutches, Mahomes found himself coming off the bench. He played his first game as the starting quarterback against the Texas Longhorns. Mahomes managed to impress his coach during that game and remained the starting quarterback.

By his sophomore year, he was already one of the greatest passers in the country, breaking records with his impressive passing yards, touchdowns, and rushing yards. During his junior year, he was awarded the Sammy Baugh Trophy for being the top passer in college football. He was also named the Scholar-Athlete of the Year.

GOING PRO

During his senior year, however, Mahomes decided to leave college behind. Instead of hitting the books, Mahomes entered the 2017 NFL draft. He was selected as the first round 10th pick by the Kansas City Chiefs. Kansas City had high expectations for the young quarterback. The general manager of the Chiefs, Brett Veach, said, “He's one of the best players I've ever seen.”

Still, during his rookie year Mahomes got little playing time. Once again, he had to be patient and work hard to earn his place in the starting lineup. And once again, he was a backup for another quarterback. This one was named Alex Smith. Mahomes became the starting quarterback at the end of the 2017 NFL season, after Smith was traded to another team.

The Chiefs were eager to recruit Mahomes to play for their team.

MORE THAN JUST A NAME

The Kansas City Chiefs are one of the best teams in football, but that doesn't mean they're perfect. Many people feel the team's name, logo, "war chant," and "tomahawk chop"—a gesture that refers to an axe used by some Indigenous peoples—are racist. The team's name is a reference to the leaders of Indigenous peoples in North America. Many find the team's arrowhead logo and "tomahawk chop" fan celebration disrespectful. "There's no respectful way to mascot us or belittle us and use us for profit," said Amanda Blackhorse, founder of Arizona to Rally Against Native Mascots.

Activist Rhonda LeValdo protests the Kansas City Chiefs' name, logo, and "tomahawk chop" in 2024.

Other sports teams have had names referring to Indigenous peoples. But most of them listened to Native American peoples and sports fans when they said their names should change. The Kansas City Chiefs haven't retired their name. The team has responded to some feedback and has worked with Indigenous communities to create a list of guidelines for Chiefs' athletes and fans. The guidelines include things like banning costume headdresses in their stadium.

For many people these changes aren't enough, and the name of Kansas City's football team is still a topic of debate.

Mahomes dives for a touchdown in a January 2019 playoff game.

Mahomes's second year as a professional football player started in 2018. It didn't take long for Kansas City to start making history and turning heads. Mahomes became the first ever Kansas City player to be named the NFL MVP. He was also named to the 2019 Pro Bowl as well as to AP's NFL All-Pro first team. He managed to lead his team to a 12–4 regular season record and the American Football Conference (AFC) Championship Game. However, Kansas City's Super Bowl dreams would have to wait, as Mahomes and the Chiefs were defeated in the playoffs by Tom Brady and the New England Patriots.

Though they didn't have a championship to show for it, Kansas City had had a terrific season. And in only two years of playing in the NFL, Mahomes was proving to be one of the greatest football players on the planet.

Mahomes warms up for a Chiefs game in October 2019.

QUICK RECOVERY

Mahomes continued to lead the Chiefs to success in his third year, pulling in another 12–4 record in 2019. But during week seven of the NFL regular season, it looked as though Mahomes's luck might be running out. During a game against the Denver Broncos, Mahomes dislocated his patella, or kneecap. It was the most serious injury he had suffered in his entire career. But that didn't stop Mahomes from wanting to play.

He begged to be put back into the game, but the team

decided against it. After getting X-rays, Mahomes made sure his family knew he was okay, and then he watched the rest of the game on a TV in the locker room. Even while his teammates beat the Broncos 30–6, they couldn't help worrying that Mahomes's season might be over. The injury had looked very bad.

After scanning his injured knee in an MRI machine, doctors said that there was no serious damage and that Mahomes would be back to the field in three weeks. When the Chiefs got Mahomes's MRI results back, they realized his timeline for returning would depend on his physical therapy. With the type of injury Mahomes had, it was important to keep the muscles in his knee moving so they didn't shut down because of swelling.

Just two days after the injury, Mahomes was already running on an underwater treadmill and planning his workout routine. He refused to miss a single team practice and could be seen stretching alongside his teammates. Even with his injury, Mahomes was spending four to five hours a day in the gym, working out.

Because Mahomes committed to his recovery and workouts straight away, he was able to avoid missing too much time. While the doctors estimated he'd be out for three weeks, Mahomes only missed two. Another person who wasn't as determined to work on their recovery might've missed a lot more time. And when he did return to the football field, he was the same Patrick Mahomes fans had come to root for, throwing touchdown passes and rushing the ball himself.

A BIG LOSS

Back on the field, the star player again led Kansas City to the AFC Championship Game. In an exciting comeback victory, Kansas City defeated the Tennessee Titans, securing their place in the 2019–2020 Super Bowl. After defeating the San Francisco 49ers to win their first Super Bowl in 50 years, Kansas City looked untouchable. Mahomes and his teammates were overjoyed, and they were looking to win another.

To start the 2020 NFL season, Mahomes signed a $500

Mahomes celebrates winning the 2020 AFC Championship Game against the Tennessee Titans, which put the Chiefs in the Super Bowl that year.

Chiefs running back Clyde Edwards-Helaire runs around a Tampa Bay player in the 2021 Super Bowl.

million contract extension to stay with the Kansas City Chiefs. Throughout the regular season, he led the team to an impressive 14–2 record. Yet again, Kansas City played their way to the Super Bowl, and yet again, Mahomes found himself facing off against Tom Brady with his new team, the Tampa Bay Buccaneers. The defending champions had their work cut out for them. Throughout the Super Bowl game, the Buccaneers played terrific defense that resulted in Mahomes being sacked three times, hit twice, and throwing multiple incomplete passes and two interceptions.

Mahomes (*right*) and teammate Travis Kelce celebrate their win against the Buffalo Bills after the AFC Championship NFL game on January 26, 2025.

DYNAMIC DUO

While Patrick Mahomes is the greatest quarterback in the NFL, no quarterback can win without a good receiver ready to catch the ball. Mahomes has a great receiver in his teammate Travis Kelce. Most NFL fans will tell you Patrick Mahomes and Travis Kelce are the greatest duo in professional football. Some might even say they're the best of all time. The pair have made history with their championship wins and playoffs success. Working together, they've combined for 1,435 yards and 16 scores in the playoffs, setting the NFL record.

It probably helps that the Chiefs' star players like each other so much. When asked by a reporter about his relationship with Kelce, Mahomes was quick to say how much the 35-year-old receiver inspires him. He called Kelce "the hardest working dude on the team" and reflected on how watching Kelce taught Mahomes to work even harder at football. They're close friends off the field, and Kelce was even a groomsman in Mahomes's wedding.

It was a brutally difficult game for Mahomes and Kansas City, and they lost to Tampa Bay 31–9. Some people called it the worst game of Mahomes's entire career. But he didn't shy away from questions after the game, saying, "They were the better team today. They beat us pretty good. The worst I think I've been beaten in a long time."

While some players might try to demand a trade or blame their teammates after such a difficult loss, Mahomes regrouped with his team and got ready to try again in the 2021 season.

MORE THAN AN ATHLETE

As if being one of the best football players in the world wasn't enough, Mahomes kept himself busy off the field as an activist during 2020. It was an important year for activism and hard conversations. The COVID-19 pandemic led to people having important conversations about how to stay healthy. But that wasn't the only big news of 2020.

On May 25, a 46-year-old Black man named George Floyd Jr. was murdered by a police officer in Minneapolis, Minnesota. This wasn't the first time police officers had harmed or killed a Black person. In the following days, the people of Minneapolis protested, and a movement spread across the nation and the entire world.

All over, people were talking about George Floyd. They protested racist policing practices and police brutality.

Mahomes was one of many celebrities who joined the conversation.

Many organizations, including professional sports leagues such as the NBA, spoke out against racism in 2020. But for a long time, the NFL was silent. Mahomes and other NFL players found this unacceptable. They knew they were living through an important moment in history, and they knew they needed to say something. Joining his teammate Tyrann Mathieu, Mahomes and other professional football players made a video asking the NFL to speak out against racism and police violence against Black people. Toward the end of the video, Mahomes looked into the camera and said, "Black lives matter."

Thousands of people joined a Black Lives Matter demonstration in New York's Times Square in June 2020.

Mahomes attends a pregame warm-up in Kansas City in September 2020.

The video was divisive. Although most people knew that racism was wrong, some people wanted Mahomes to stop talking about social issues and just play football. But the superstar quarterback wasn't worried about what those people thought, saying, "I'm going to do whatever I can to fight for equality for all people. And I feel like I've shown that over this offseason and I'm going to continue that fight. I'm not worried about people and how they're going to do negative stuff back to me. I'm worried about doing what's right for humanity and making sure all people feel equal."

The video succeeded in its mission. Shortly after the players created it, both the NFL and the Kansas City Chiefs gave statements saying they supported the players and the Black community. More important, it helped the nation focus on a critical social justice issue.

Mahomes plays in a 2019 celebrity softball game to help raise money for a Kansas City children's hospital.

In addition to fighting for racial equality, Mahomes spent a lot of time encouraging people to vote in the 2020 US presidential election. Once again teaming up with fellow activist Tyrann Mathieu, Mahomes started a voter registration project in Kansas City. Teammates on and off the field, Mathieu and Mahomes encouraged people to get out and vote.

Mahomes also joined with basketball legend LeBron James to encourage people to register to vote and to cast their votes. They educated people on how to vote and why their vote mattered. They also focused on teaching people how to overcome voter suppression.

Leading up to the 2020 US presidential election, some states passed strict voting laws that made it hard for voters to register and cast their votes. These voting laws often affected lower-income communities and racially

15 AND THE MAHOMIES

Mahomes had a big year in 2019. In addition to having an incredible football season, he founded a nonprofit organization called 15 and the Mahomies Foundation, focused on improving the lives of children. The organization offers programs that promote reading, support educational success, and encourage young people to get out and volunteer in their communities. The foundation also partners with many charities, including Lead to Read KC and the Make-A-Wish Foundation.

Outside of its official programs and partnerships, 15 and the Mahomies raises money for charity, providing things such as meals and winter clothes to families in need of support. They hosted a celebrity gala for charity that was attended by celebrities including Taylor Swift and have donated millions of dollars to other charities.

diverse neighborhoods. When asked about their efforts to educate people on voting, James said, "Yes, we want you to go out and vote, but we're also going to give you the tutorial. We're going to give you the background of how to vote and what they're trying to do, the other side, to stop you from voting."

Mahomes's foundation, 15 and the Mahomies, even split the cost of new voting machines with the Kansas City Chiefs to make sure everyone in the city was able to cast their vote.

On and off the field, Mahomes's actions make a huge impact. While he's one of the greatest athletes on the planet, he continues to show his fans, and the world, that he cares about much more than just football.

MAKING HISTORY

Kansas City didn't make the Super Bowl in 2021. That year, the team was focused on getting even better. Working with the team, Mahomes changed his payment deal.

The NFL has rules about how much teams can spend on player salaries. Mahomes agreed to get some of his pay in bonuses at different times. Bonuses aren't included in those NFL pay limits. Doing this meant the team could spend an extra $16 million on signing new players.

While the Chiefs made it to the AFC Championship Game again, they ended up losing to the Cincinnati Bengals, with Mahomes throwing two interceptions. But that didn't discourage Mahomes or Kansas City. After a couple of hard years of losing important games, Mahomes and Kansas City were ready to take over the league in the 2022 NFL regular season.

And they did. Mahomes had an incredible season, leading his team to a strong 14–3 regular season record. While football is a team sport, where every player, coach, and trainer has a role to play, much of Kansas City's success that year was thanks to Mahomes.

During the 2022 season, his 5,608 total yards (passed

Tampa Bay linebacker Jason Pierre-Paul tries to tackle Mahomes in the 2021 Super Bowl.

and rushed) broke the NFL record for total yards in one season by a quarterback. He set Kansas City's franchise record for most passing yards in a season with an impressive 5,250 yards. The same year, he reached an all-time total of 12 rushing touchdowns. That was a new franchise record.

Even though he sprained his ankle during a game against the Jacksonville Jaguars, Mahomes led his team to victory after victory throughout the AFC tournament. With his clever passing, Kansas City defeated the Cincinnati Bengals, winning the AFC Championship and securing their place in the 2022 Super Bowl. It was a hard-fought game against the Philadelphia Eagles, with both teams scoring plenty of touchdowns.

GOLFER

Patrick Mahomes will likely go down as one of the greatest football players of all time, and many people know about his past as a basketball player and a baseball player. But not everyone knows Mahomes also enjoys a secret fourth sport! When he isn't throwing perfect passes to his teammates or spending time with his wife and kids, Mahomes likes to be on the golf course. Sometimes he even golfs with teammates, including Travis Kelce.

Mahomes enjoys golf so much that he played in a celebrity golf competition called The Match. In the competition, Mahomes and Kelce found themselves competing against professional basketball players Stephen Curry and Klay Thompson. Mahomes and Kelce managed to beat the pair, even though Curry is known for his skill as a golfer.

When asked about the win, Mahomes credited it to teamwork, saying, "Steph's a great golfer, I thought Klay did a good job out there today. But they didn't have that team aspect that we had."

Mahomes takes a practice swing at a Las Vegas golf course in 2022.

But when Kansas City went into the halftime break, they found themselves down by 10 points. The score was 14–24. Even worse, they had an injured star: Mahomes had reinjured his sprained ankle.

Playing through the pain, Mahomes stayed in the game, leading Kansas City to touchdown after touchdown. By continuing to play, Mahomes ran the risk of making his injury far worse. But he did throw two touchdowns in the fourth quarter, and with five minutes left in the game, Kansas City managed to tie the score 35–35. With eight seconds left on the clock, Harrison Butker kicked a 27-yard field goal to win the game. The final score was 38–35.

Mahomes (*upper left*) throws a pass in the 2023 Super Bowl game against the Eagles.

Mahomes flashes a grin following the Chiefs' 2023 Super Bowl victory.

Again, Kansas City had won the Super Bowl, and again, Patrick Mahomes had earned the Super Bowl MVP award. He also earned the regular season MVP award, in addition to being the league leader in passing yards and passing touchdowns. He was the first player in NFL history to achieve all four accomplishments in one season.

When a sports commentator asked him how it felt to win his second Super Bowl, Mahomes said it hadn't really sunk in yet. Then he said, "The failure of the last two years of losing in the Super Bowl and losing in an AFC

Championship Game, this one hits different. The first one it was all like happy go lucky, everything like that. This one, you appreciate the hard work that it took to get here."

After falling short of their championship dreams two years in a row, Mahomes had led Kansas City back to a Super Bowl victory. The superstar quarterback had even broken NFL records along the way! But he wasn't done yet, and neither were the Kansas City Chiefs.

ALL EYES ON KANSAS CITY

At the start of the 2023 NFL regular season, all eyes were on Kansas City. Everyone wondered if they'd be able to pull off another Super Bowl win and establish themselves as a football dynasty. Only a championship would do. To be called a dynasty, a sports team needs to win their league's championship many times in a row. But before they could worry about winning the Super Bowl, Kansas City had to battle their way to the playoffs once again.

Mahomes's ankle was able to heal during the offseason, and he came into the 2023 regular season ready to make even more history. In just the fourth week of the season, Mahomes threw a pass for his 200th career touchdown, reaching that milestone faster than anyone before him. By defeating the Minnesota Vikings in the following week, he became the youngest player of all time, at age 28, to beat every other NFL team.

Mahomes celebrates with his wife and children after winning the 2024 Super Bowl against the San Francisco 49ers.

FAMILY MAN

In 2021 Mahomes and Brittany Matthews, his high school girlfriend, welcomed their first child, a daughter, Sterling Mahomes. In 2022 the couple married and their son Patrick Mahomes III, nicknamed Bronze, was born. Then, in 2025, they welcomed their third child and second daughter, Golden Mahomes. In addition to their three children, the Mahomes family has two dogs, Silver and Steel.

While everyone knows Mahomes loves playing football, his family is the one thing Mahomes loves even more. In an interview with *Time* magazine, Mahomes said that if he ever feels like football is taking away from his family time, he'll know it's time to go. Mahomes brings his kids to watch his games and celebrate his Super Bowl victories.

Mahomes also has a close relationship with his parents. The two often appear at their son's games, cheering him on.

Mahomes starts a play in a 2023 game against the Cincinnati Bengals.

Although Mahomes broke records early, the season was definitely not easy. More of Mahomes's passes got intercepted than normal, and his passing yards per game were lower than usual. Kansas City struggled at first, especially their receivers, who were dropping passes left and right. Eventually the team figured things out, finishing with a strong 11–6 season.

Despite their early struggles, they played well enough to make it to the playoffs once again, where they defeated the Miami Dolphins, Buffalo Bills, and Baltimore Ravens. After beating the Ravens in the AFC Championship Game, Kansas City had once again played their way to the Super Bowl, where they would have a rematch with the San Francisco 49ers.

Just like their previous Super Bowl matchup in 2020, the 49ers played hard and built up an early lead. Going into halftime, Kansas City was losing 10–3. With Mahomes throwing perfectly aimed passes to his ready receivers, Kansas City managed to fight their way back

Mahomes runs past 49ers safety Logan Ryan in the 2024 Super Bowl game.

into the game. When the whistle blew and the fourth quarter ended, the score was tied 19–19.

For the second time in NFL history, the Super Bowl was going into overtime. The 49ers scored three points on a successful field goal kick in the first possession of overtime. But Mahomes stayed calm, throwing the game-winning touchdown pass to Mecole Hardman. The final score was 25–22.

Mahomes had won his third championship in Kansas City and his second championship in a row. No one had won the Super Bowl two years in a row since the New

Mahomes holds up the Vince Lombardi Trophy after the Chiefs' 2024 Super Bowl win.

England Patriots in 2005. For the second year in a row, Mahomes was named the Super Bowl MVP. He was the third player in NFL history to win three Super Bowl MVPs.

Mahomes holds the Super Bowl LVIII MVP trophy at a press conference in 2024.

THREE IN A ROW?

Going into the 2024–2025 regular season, the future was looking bright for Kansas City. Because they'd won their last two Super Bowls, they were in a position to make history by being the first team to ever win three Super Bowls in a row.

Mahomes and the Chiefs didn't waste any time. Throughout the regular season, they led the NFL with an impressive 15–2 record. To many football fans, Kansas City seemed like the clear favorite to win it all once again.

After playing their way to the Super Bowl, Mahomes became the first quarterback in NFL history to start in five Super Bowls before turning 30 years old. But it wasn't time to celebrate just yet.

Mahomes and the Chiefs would face off against star quarterback Jalen Hurts and the Philadelphia Eagles. The

Eagles, known for their impressive defense, were coming off a strong 14–3 season. They weren't going to make things easy for Mahomes. The Eagles were ready to take on the Chiefs and earn their second Super Bowl win.

On February 9, 2025, football fans and celebrities crowded into Caesars Superdome in New Orleans to watch Super Bowl LIX. It didn't take long for fans around the world to realize this wasn't going to be an easy win for Kansas City.

Jalen Hurts (*center*) scores a touchdown against the Chiefs in the 2025 Super Bowl.

Mahomes congratulates Hurts after the Eagles' 2025 Super Bowl win.

The Eagles came out strong, scoring touchdown after touchdown, and for once, the Chiefs didn't seem to have any answers. They went into halftime down 0–24. Mahomes had thrown two interceptions that cost his team dearly. The crushing defense the Eagles were known for was proving too strong to overcome.

In the second half, Mahomes was able to turn things around and the Chiefs began to score. But this time, his quarterback magic wasn't enough to save the day.

The final score was 40–22. Silver confetti fell to the field as the Eagles celebrated their victory. Kansas City's Super Bowl dreams had come to an end, along with their dreams of the first-ever NFL three-peat, or winning three times in a row.

After the game, Mahomes took full responsibility for the loss, saying, "I didn't play to my standard, and I have to be better next time." Even though the season didn't end as they'd planned, the Kansas City Chiefs had already made history as one of the greatest NFL teams of all time. And, surprising no one, Mahomes didn't let the loss define him or his career. He got back to work.

Mahomes has broken record after record and won Kansas City an impressive number of championships. When he's not leading Kansas City to the Super Bowl, Mahomes continues to use his voice to encourage people to vote and to advocate for racial equality. The superstar quarterback has much of his career ahead of him, and there's no telling how much he'll accomplish by the end of it. From breaking records to winning championships and leading his team into the history books, Mahomes seems poised to keep wowing his fans for many years to come.

IMPORTANT DATES

1995 Patrick Mahomes II is born on September 17.

2014 Mahomes graduates from Whitehouse High School.

He is drafted to play baseball for the Detroit Tigers, an offer he declines.

2017 Mahomes is drafted into the NFL on April 27.

2019 Mahomes announces the 15 and the Mahomies Foundation.

Mahomes dislocates his kneecap in October.

He returns from his kneecap injury on November 10, ahead of schedule.

2020 He wins his first Super Bowl and first Super Bowl MVP award on February 2.

Mahomes and other players make a video asking the NFL to speak out against racism.

2021 Kansas City loses to Tampa Bay in the Super Bowl on February 7.

Sterling Mahomes is born on February 20.

2022 Patrick Mahomes marries Brittany Matthews on March 12.

Patrick "Bronze" Mahomes III is born on November 28.

2023 Mahomes wins his second Super Bowl and his second Super Bowl MVP award on February 12.

2024 Mahomes wins his third Super Bowl and his third Super Bowl MVP award on February 11.

2025 Golden Mahomes is born on January 13.

The Philadelphia Eagles defeat the Kansas City Chiefs in Super Bowl LIX.

SOURCE NOTES

7 Associated Press, "Mahomes Leads Chiefs' Rally Past 49ers in Super Bowl, 31–20," *ESPN*, February 3, 2020, https://www.espn.com/nfl/recap/_/gameId/401131047.

10 "Patrick Mahomes Wins MVP of Super Bowl LIV," video, 1:19, posted by Kansas City Chiefs, accessed January 22, 2025, https://www.chiefs.com/video/patrick-mahomes-wins-mvp-of-super-bowl-liv.

13 Ilana Frost, "All About Patrick Mahomes' Parents, Pat Mahomes and Randi Martin," *People*, January 22, 2025, https://people.com/sports/all-about-patrick-mahomes-parents/.

15 Adam Teicher, "Brett Veach on Patrick Mahomes II: 'One of the Best I've Ever Seen,'" *ESPN*, March 1, 2018, https://www.espn.com/blog/kansas-city-chiefs/post/_/id/24182/brett-veach-on-patrick-mahomes-ii-one-of-the-best-ive-ever-seen.

16 Deena Zaru and Nakylah Carter, "Native American Advocates Protest Kansas City Chiefs Name Ahead of Super Bowl LVII," ABC News, February 12, 2023, https://abcnews.go.com/ABCNews/native-american-advocates-protest-kansas-city-chiefs-ahead/story?id=97068258.

22 Sean Neumann, "Patrick Mahomes Gushes over Travis Kelce After Another Chiefs Win: 'He Means the World to Me,'" *People*, December 9, 2024, https://people.com/patrick-mahomes-gushes-travis-kelce-means-the-world-to-me-8758157.

23 Adam Teicher, "Patrick Mahomes Says Super Bowl LV Loss Was 'Worst I've Been Beaten in Long Time,'" *ESPN*, February 8, 2021, https://www.espn.com/nfl/story/_/id/30858806/patrick-mahomes-says-super-bowl-lv-loss-was-worst-beaten-long.

24 "#StrongerTogether," Facebook video, posted by Patrick Mahomes, June 5, 2020, https://www.facebook.com/watch/?v=1205130866495653.

25 Braulio Perez, "Patrick Mahomes Has the Perfect Answer for Fans Against BLM Movement," Fansided, August 29, 2020, https://fansided.com/2020/08/29/patrick-mahomes-answer-chiefs-fans-blm-movement/.

27 Joshua Brisco, "Patrick Mahomes Unites with LeBron James' 'More Than a Vote' Campaign," *Sports Illustrated*, June 23, 2020, https://www.si.com/nfl/chiefs/news/patrick-mahomes-unites-with-lebron-james-more-than-a-vote-campaign.

30 Mike Florio, "Patrick Mahomes, Travis Kelce Win Celebrity Golf Match Against Steph Curry, Klay Thompson," NBC Sports, June 30, 2023, https://www.nbcsports.com/nfl/profootballtalk/rumor-mill/news/patrick-mahomes-travis-kelce-win-celebrity-golf-match-against-steph-curry-klay-thompson.

32–33 "Patrick Mahomes Reacts to Winning His 2nd Super Bowl MVP: NFL Primetime," YouTube video, 5:37, posted by *ESPN*, February 12, 2023, https://www.youtube.com/watch?v=6apcXU4lz8c.

41 Matt McMullen, "Chiefs Fall to Eagles, 40–22, in Super Bowl LIX," Chiefs, February 10, 2025, https://www.chiefs.com/news/chiefs-fall-to-eagles-40-22-in-super-bowl-lix.

SELECTED BIBLIOGRAPHY

Augustyn, Adam. "Kansas City Chiefs." *Britannica*. Updated January 20, 2025. https://www.britannica.com/topic/Kansas-City-Chiefs.

Bishop, Greg. "Patrick Mahomes and Travis Kelce Are More Than the NFL's Greatest Dynamic Duo." *Sports Illustrated*, January 24, 2024. https://www.si.com/nfl/2024/01/24/patrick-mahomes-travis-kelce-greatest-dynamic-duo-chiefs-playoffs.

Brisco, Joshua. "Patrick Mahomes Unites with LeBron James' 'More Than a Vote' Campaign." *Sports Illustrated*, June 23, 2020. https://www.si.com/nfl/chiefs/news/patrick-mahomes-unites-with-lebron-james-more-than-a-vote-campaign.

Gardner, Steve, Safid Deen, and Chris Bumbaca. "Super Bowl 57 Final Score: Chiefs Top Eagles 38–35 Thanks to Late-Game Magic from Mahomes." *USA Today*, February 12, 2023. https://www.usatoday.com/story/sports/nfl/super-bowl/2023/02/12/super-bowl-2023-live-updates-chiefs-eagles/11218626002/.

Hudgins, Ryan. "Meet NFL Star Patrick Mahomes' Dad: 5 Things to Know About Patrick Mahomes Sr." *US Weekly*, August 27, 2024. https://www.usmagazine.com/celebrity-moms/news/everything-to-know-about-patrick-mahomes-dad-patrick-mahomes-sr/.

Lakritz, Talia, and Max Kalnitz. "18 Things You May Not Have Known About Patrick Mahomes." *Business Insider*, February 11, 2024. https://www.businessinsider.com/patrick-mahomes-things-to-know-2021-2.

Patra, Kevin. "MRI Confirms Patrick Mahomes Out at Least 3 Weeks." NFL, October 18, 2019. https://www.nfl.com/news/mri-confirms-patrick-mahomes-out-at-least-3-weeks-0ap3000001066803.

"Patrick Mahomes Wins MVP of Super Bowl LIV." Video, 1:19. Chiefs. Accessed January 22, 2025. https://www.chiefs.com/video/patrick-mahomes-wins-mvp-of-super-bowl-liv.

Vita, Jack. "Chiefs' Patrick Mahomes Was Drafted by Detroit Tigers in 2014 MLB Draft." *Sports Illustrated*, February 2, 2023. https://www.si.com/fannation/mlb/fastball/news/chiefs-patrick-mahomes-was-drafted-by-detroit-tigers-in-2014-mlb-draft.

Zaru, Deena, and Nakylah Carter. "Native American Advocates Protest Kansas City Chiefs Name Ahead of Super Bowl LVII." ABC News, February 12, 2023. https://abcnews.go.com/ABCNews/native-american-advocates-protest-kansas-city-chiefs-ahead/story?id=97068258.

LEARN MORE

Adamson, Thomas K. *Travis Kelce*. Bellwether Media, 2025.

Britannica Kids: Patrick Mahomes
https://kids.britannica.com/students/article/PatrickMahomes/632146

Dolan, Hannah. *Patrick Mahomes*. Welbeck Children's Books, 2024.

Kiddle: Patrick Mahomes Facts for Kids
https://kids.kiddle.co/Patrick_Mahomes

Kidz Search: Patrick Mahomes
https://wiki.kidzsearch.com/wiki/Patrick_Mahomes

Levit, Joe. *Meet Patrick Mahomes*. Lerner Publications, 2023.

INDEX

PHOTO ACKNOWLEDGMENTS

Image credits: AP Photo/Brooke Sutton, p. 2; AP Photo/Scott Boehm, p. 6; AP Photo/Perry Knotts, p. 8; AP Photo/Ryan Kang, p. 9; Mitchell Layton/Getty Images, p. 11; AP Photo/Jerod Foster/Icon Sportswire, p. 12; AP Photo/Ron Jenkins, p. 14; Rich Graessle/Icon Sportswire/Getty Images, p. 15; AP Photo/Ed Zurga, p. 16; AP Photo/Tom DiPace, p. 17; AP Photo/Aaron M. Sprecher, p. 18, 28; AP Photo/Colin E. Braley, p. 20; AP Photo/Ben Liebenberg, p. 21; AP Photo/Joe Robbins, p. 22; AP Photo/Michael Nigro/Sipa USA, p. 24; AP Photo/Steve Sanders/Kansas City Chiefs, p. 25; Kyle Rivas/Getty Images, p. 26; AP Photo/Ashley Landis, p. 29; Carmen Mandato/Getty Images, p. 30; AP Photo/Adam Bow/Icon Sportswire, p. 31; AP Photo/Matt Slocum, p. 32; AP Photo/Perry Knotts, p. 34; AP Photo/Peter Aiken, p. 35; AP Photo/George Walker IV, p. 36; AP Photo/Doug Benc, p. 37; AP Photo/Godofredo A. Vásquez, p. 39; AP Photo/Adam Hunger, p. 40.

Cover: AP Photo/Brooke Sutton; fotograzia/Getty Images.